Where Is the Cat?

by Sam Baker

PEARSON

Glenview, Illinois • Boston, Massachusetts
Chandler, Arizona • Upper Saddle River, New Jersey

Where is the cat?

in a tree

Where is the cat?

I see a cat!

Where is the cat?

in a bag

Where is the cat?